herbs & spi

all about ginger, chives & garlic

by Colin West

Visit my website at howtogrowherbgarden.com

Individual Books in the Series:

#1 Herbs & Spices – all about ginger

#2 Herbs & Spices – all about chives

#3 Herbs & Spices – all about garlic

TABLE OF CONTENTS

1 - Introduction to Ginger

Section 1of this compilation is dedicated to one of the greatest and most popular spices and one of my particular favorites – **ginger**, a wonderfully versatile and rather weird looking tuber, known botanically as *zingiber officinale*.

As a member of the plant family *zingiberaceae* therefore it is related to turmeric and cardamom.

Ginger is a fiery knobbly root with rough beige skin and hard, juicy, pale yellow skin. Ginger root is actually a rhizome or 'underground stem'.

The somewhat fibrous flesh is creamy white to pale yellow in color, depending on the variety.

Ginger can be used as a spice, fresh or dried and ground to a powder. The fresh, juicy root has a sweetly pungent taste and a perfume-like scent that makes it suitable for sweet or savoury dishes.

Young ginger can also be preserved in sugar syrup or crystallized and rolled in sugar - it is then known as stem ginger.

One quick point of clarity – we tend to talk about ginger root when talking about the edible part of the ginger plant, which is actually technically incorrect.

You eat the rhizomes, and as you can see, rhizomes have roots... two different things, but I'll keep talking about ginger root anyway, that's what everybody does and now you know what I mean.

And to whet your appetite and get you busy enjoying ginger - I have selected 10 of my favourite recipes which use ginger as a key ingredient. These feature at the end of the section.

For many centuries, **ginger** has been consumed in countries all around the world. It has been widely used as a spice and is commonly used as a delicacy.

Not only is **ginger** a delightful snack or addition to various meals and savouries, it also has many proven medicinal purposes, which can also be dated back to ancient times.

Ginger can be used as a food preservative. It has also been proven to destroy harmful bacteria, such as salmonella.

With all of the uses for this plant, ginger has become extraordinarily popular over the years for household uses as well as for natural health remedies.

Ginger was originally cultivated in Asia, where it is still very common in local dishes, but is now grown widely in West Africa, the Caribbean, India, Europe, South America, and North America.

Ginger characteristically has a mild taste and is rather juicy. However, the roots of the plant are very fibrous and almost completely dry.

The taste and smell of **ginger** can be attributed to the mixture of zingerone, gingerols, and shogaols, which are the oils that comprise 1 to 3 percent of Ginger's weight when fresh.

Ginger also contains nearly 3 percent of fragrant and essential oils.

The Uses of Ginger

Fresh **ginger** can add spice, heat and flavor to a great variety of dishes, including meats, vegetables, fruits and even sweets. Ginger root is typically sold in 3 to 8 inch pieces, and you will easily find it in your local grocery store.

Ginger is used in Asian medicine to treat stomach aches, nausea, and diarrhea. Many digestive, anti-nausea, and cold and flu dietary supplements sold in the United States contain ginger extract as an ingredient.

Ginger is also used to ease the discomfort of rheumatoid arthritis, osteoarthritis, and joint and muscle pain.

The underground stems of the ginger plant are also used in cooking, baking, and for health purposes. Common forms of ginger include fresh or dried root, tablets, capsules, liquid extracts (tinctures), and teas.

Freezing your own **ginger** is a great way of ensuring an always available food ingredient – but with the flavor of fresh spice. You don't need to wrap when you store it in the freezer.

You can then borrow it from the freezer and grate directly into dishes frozen, or break off a quantity to use as desired.

Ginger as Medicine

Ginger has many medicinal purposes and it is frequently used as a natural home remedy for many ailments.

Ginger can aid gastrointestinal tract regulation, and it is considered to have analgesic, antibacterial, and sedative properties when consumed regularly as part of a healthy, daily diet.

For thousands of years, herbalists have used the root of the ginger plant to relieve stomach troubles.

With its natural anti-inflammatory effects, **ginger** is also a common remedy for inflammation-related health problems like arthritis.

Ginger can also perform a sialogoue action, which means it will stimulate saliva production and ease swallowing difficulties.

The rhizomes and stems of ginger have played significant roles in Chinese, Japanese, and Indian medicine since the 1500s.

The oleoresin of **ginger** is often contained in digestive, antiflatulent, laxative, and antacid compounds.

Ginger has, in studies, also demonstrated that it is capable of killing ovarian cancer cells, as well as certain forms of skin cancer.

Side effects such as gas, bloating, and heartburn are most often associated with powdered ginger.

Growing Ginger at Home

Ginger is a beautiful looking and beautifully scented plant. You can easily grow a year's supply of ginger root from your first tubers.

And after a year or two you will start to have enough to give away both to your friends to eat or plant.

Whether growing in a container or in your garden you can get your first fresh ginger roots at a local store or an Asian market.

Better still ask a fellow grower for a few rhizomes. Look for chunky fat tubers (4-6 inches long) with plenty of growth buds or knobs - pieces with well developed "eyes".

Cut the rhizome into one or two 2-inch pieces. The growth buds are where the shoots will emerge. Wait a few days to let the cut ends dry out and harden off before planting.

Whether you grow your **ginger** root in a pot or in the ground, you need good soil to start with.

Ginger needs to be rich enough to feed your ginger and to hold enough moisture so it doesn't dry out, but it needs to be free draining so the ginger roots don't become waterlogged.

A sheltered, moist spot in a warm climate will provide enough humidity. If you have problems with dry air then regular spraying and misting might help.

Ginger can be grown in temperate climates during the warm summer months, where the ginger plant dies back during the fall and is dormant in winter even when it is brought inside the house.

Ginger Likes:

A rich moist soil

Good shelter

Warm weather

Ginger Dislikes:

Frost

Direct sunlight

Soggy, waterlogged soil

Strong winds

Growing Ginger in a Container

1. Use a pot or container that's about a foot across and a foot deep, and has excellent drainage at the bottom. This will take 3 good sized tubers comfortably. Use a pot large enough to allow the rhizome to grow.

2. Fill the container three quarters full with potting soil enriched with plenty of natural compost.

3. Soak the tubers in warm water overnight, then set them in the pot just below the soil surface, spacing them evenly, with the buds facing up.

4. Put the container in a light shaded area, indoors or out, depending on the temperature at the time.

5. Water only sparingly at first, too much moisture in the beginning may cause the rhizome to rot. Water more generously when growth starts.

6. Move plants outside only if temperatures have reached 50 degrees F. Keep inside in cooler weather, otherwise growth can be stunted.

7. If started outside, shield the plants from high winds, and move them indoors at the first sign of cool temperatures.

8. Plants reach maturity at a height of 2 - 4 feet, in 10 months to a year, depending on soil quality and attention.

9. Pull out plants carefully when new, young sprouts that appear in front of the main plants will hopefully form their own tubers; use what you need, and freeze or replant the rest in fresh compost.

10. Clip the young, tender stems any time.

Growing Ginger in the Garden

1. If you live in a colder climate - start your ginger indoors, it will be too cold outside in spring. (See Container Tips).

2. Plant ginger outside in early spring for best results, when you have warm enough temperatures outside. The dormant tubers will sprout only when the temperature reaches 75 to 85 degrees Fahrenheit.

3. Choose a sheltered, lightly shaded site (not direct sun), with rich, moist but well-drained soil. Work in plenty of compost to ensure the right base. If the ground is moist and warm ginger will root easily. I use a mix of 1 part compost to 1 part of my sandy garden soil. The compost supplies the nutrition and holds water, and the sand makes sure the mix drains freely.

4. If your garden has good soil just dig in some compost and that should be good enough. If your soil is too heavy you can make a raised bed, or a small ridge to improve drainage. The soil should never dry out. Don't overwater, though, because the water that drains away will take nutrients with it.

5. If starting outside - snap or break up the ginger rhizomes in little pieces with a couple of growing buds each. Or just plant the whole thing. Plant your ginger root five to ten centimetres deep, with the growing buds facing up.

6. Ginger doesn't take up much room. Every rhizome you plant will first only grow a few leaves, in the one spot. Over time it will become a dense clump and slowly get bigger, but only if it isn't harvested. The rhizomes underground don't mind if they become a bit crowded.

7. It is a good idea to mulch the ground after planting. The ginger plant grows from a creeping rhizome that sends up shoots of new growth. It helps to keep the ground moist,

it helps feed the ginger as the mulch breaks down, and it also keeps down weeds.

8. Ginger grows to a height of approximately 2 to 4 feet, with long slender leaves and small yellowish-green fragrant flowers with dark purple markings.

9. The aerial parts of the ginger plant (flowers, stems, and leaves) are not generally used in cooking or in medicines.

10. The rhizome is ready for harvesting when it is about 4 to 6 inches in length, usually after 6 to 8 months. If you cultivate ginger in the spring it can be harvested in the fall, when the foliage naturally dies back as the weather starts cooling down.

11. If desired, rhizomes can be harvested earlier when they are smaller because size does not affect flavor. Reduce the water, and even let the ground dry out. This encourages the ginger to form stronger rhizomes. Once all the leaves have died down your ginger is ready for harvesting.

CW Note:

Ginger is slow growing, and may be overgrown by other plants in the garden. If you are growing ginger in good, rich soil it shouldn't need anything extra. I put in fresh compost mix every year and never add any extra fertilizer. If you don't have good soil, or if you are growing ginger in some standard bought potting mix, then you have to feed it regularly.

Ginger Harvesting Tips

1. If you are growing ginger root in the garden you can start stealing little bits of it once it is about four months old. Just dig carefully at the side of a clump. (This 'green' ginger does have less flavour than the mature stuff, though.)

2. The best time to harvest ginger is any time after the leaves have died down. Usually it takes 8 to 10 months to get to that point.

3. Dig the rhizome up and remove the stem and leaves. Rinse it with water and allow it to thoroughly dry in the sun (if possible).

4. You can then dig up the whole plant. The reason that I grow my ginger in containers is that it makes the harvest so easy. I don't have to dig, I just tip out the whole thing.

5. Break up the rhizomes, select a few nice ones with good buds for replanting (you can replant straight away), keep the rest for the kitchen.

6. Chop and freeze most of the herb. Another way is to cut the ginger into small chunks and store it in brandy. Alternatively store the rhizome in a plastic bag in the refrigerator, where it will keep for several weeks.

7. The rhizomes that have been replanted or left in the ground don't need any water or attention until the weather warms up again. Mine still get watered where they are, and that doesn't seem to hurt them either.

8. The other way to grow and harvest ginger is to have many clumps growing around your place, and to just dig up what you need, when you need it. Once a clump is big enough you can harvest the mature tubers without damaging new shoots.

9. Try to resist the urge to harvest all of it in the first year. Build up a good resource stock. Start by leaving at least

one rhizome and only dig it up for the first time after two years. Replant every promising looking bud and you should still have some to eat.

10. You can even grow ginger as an ornamental plant. It is very pretty with its glossy strap leaves, and it smells beautiful when you brush against it.

.. and finally (ginger)

When growing ginger as outlined above you won't see any flowers. A clump needs to be about two years old to flower. So if you want to see your ginger flower fully leave it in the ground, and just dig very carefully at the edges to harvest bits here and there.

The flowers of culinary ginger are green and insignificant anyway. However the ginger flower itself is edible, and in Asia it is used to flavor stocks and curries.

Just cut away the hard petals and eat the bud itself. Make sure to blend it or chop really finely as the plant is very hard, and could be uncomfortable to swallow, but it lends a beautiful high note to your spicy/sour base dishes that is quite unique.

Enough talking about **ginger**, now for the food!

My Top 10 Recipes With Ginger

Fresh **ginger** can be chopped, minced, grated or sliced into thin "matchsticks." Some recipes will specify how to prepare the ginger as a part of the measuring instructions. Use larger pieces, like matchsticks, when you want the bright flavor and chewy texture of ginger. A smaller chop or mince works well for many recipes, while grated ginger is ideal for anything with a smooth texture.

Many recipes measure fresh ginger by calling for a length of ginger root. You may see "one inch **ginger** root, minced" in a recipe, for instance.

If your ginger root is especially small or large, you may want to adjust the recommended amount of ginger accordingly. Thicker ginger roots may be more fibrous. If you are working with a larger root, opt for a shorter length and a finer chop or grate.

If you have grated fresh ginger or have already minced or chopped ginger, measure it by the teaspoon or tablespoon.

You can also purchase minced or grated ginger in jars or tubes at specialty food markets. One tablespoon of ginger is equal to one inch of fresh ginger root, chopped.

If you do not have fresh or jarred ginger, dried ground ginger may be substituted, with somewhat different results. Replace the ginger in the recipe with one and a half teaspoons of ground ginger, plus half a teaspoon of lemon juice.

1. Ginger Peppered Steak

Tenderize your steak dinner with a recipe that takes little time and utilizes ginger to its fullest flavor. Spice up your steak! Serves 4.

Preparation	Cooking	Serving
15 mins	15 mins	30 mins

INGREDIENTS

2 tsp sugar

2 tsp cornstarch

1/4 tsp ground ginger

1/4 cup soy sauce

1 tbsp white wine vinegar

1 pound beef flank steak, thinly sliced

2 medium green peppers, julienned (matchsticks!)

1 tsp vegetable oil

PREPARATION

In a large bowl, combine the sugar, cornstarch, ginger, soy sauce and vinegar until the mix is smooth.

Add the beef and toss to coat; set aside.

In a large skillet or wok, stir-fry the green peppers in oil until crisp-tender, about 3 minutes.

Remove with a slotted spoon and keep warm.

Add beef with marinade to pan.

Stir-fry for 3 minutes or until meat reaches desired state.

Return peppers to pan.

Heat through.

SERVING

Serve over rice (steamed or boiled) or if you prefer with fried or mashed potatoes.

2. Steamed Fish with Ginger

If you love eating fish as I do – then this authentic Chinese recipe will blow you away. Actually this is quite simple to cook, and really flavorsome. Serves 4.

Preparation	Cooking	Serving
20 mins	10 mins	30 mins

INGREDIENTS

2 pound halibut fillet (or similar fish)

2 tsp coarse sea salt (ideally)

2 tbsp minced fresh ginger, or freshly chopped

2 thinly sliced fresh onions

2 tbsp dark soy sauce

2 tbsp peanut oil

3 tsp toasted sesame oil

1/2 cup lightly packed fresh cilantro sprigs, or similar

PREPARATION

Pat halibut dry with paper towels.

Rub both sides of fillet with salt.

Scatter the ginger over the top of the fish and place onto a heatproof ceramic dish.

Place into a (bamboo) steamer over several inches of gently boiling water, and cover.

Gently steam for 10 minutes.

Pour water from dish and sprinkle fillet with green onion.

Drizzle soy sauce over the surface of the fish.

Heat peanut and sesame oils in a small skillet over medium-high heat until they begin to smoke.

When oil is hot, pour on top of the fillet.

The very hot oil will cause the onions and water on top of the fish to pop and spatter all over - be careful.

Garnish with cilantro sprigs and serve immediately.

SERVING

Garnish with cilantro sprigs.

Serve immediately with pre-prepared rice.

3. Murgh Adraki

The warmth and fragrance of ginger (adraki) is at the heart of this classic north Indian dish. Takes a bit of preparation so use on special occasion! Serves 4.

Preparation	Cooking	Serving
30 mins	60-100 mins	90-130 mins

INGREDIENTS

the chutney

2½ tbsp rapeseed oil

1 tsp cumin seeds, 2 tsp sesame seeds

200g/7oz ginger, thinly sliced

1 green chilli, slit open, 1 red chilli (or equiv. chilli powder)

100g/3½oz palm sugar

100g/3½oz tamarind paste

1 pinch asafoetida, 1 dried red chilli

½ tsp mustard seeds, 5-6 curry leaves

the chicken

4 chicken breasts, skin on

300g/10½oz chicken breast, minced

1 spring onion, chopped

2 tbsp ginger, finely chopped

1 pinch garam masala (or thai 7 spice)

1 litre/1¾ pints chicken stock

vegetable oil, for frying

the sauce

2 tbsp rapeseed oil

1 tsp cumin seeds

50g/1¾oz ginger, finely chopped

1 green chilli, slit open

2 medium onions, finely chopped

1 tsp red chilli powder

2 tsp ground coriander

1 tsp ground turmeric

2 medium tomatoes, chopped

PREPARATION

the chutney

Heat 2 tablespoons of oil in a frying pan, fry the cumin seeds for 1-2 minutes.

Add the sesame seeds, ginger and green chilli and season with a little salt.

Stir for 2-3 minutes and then cover the mixture with a circle of greaseproof paper and let it cook slowly for 40 minutes until the ginger is cooked.

Let the mixture cool then transfer to a food processor and blend to a fine paste adding the tamarind paste and palm sugar.

Heat remaining oil in separate pan, add asafoetida, red chilli, mustard seeds.

As the mustard seeds pop, add the curry leaves, stir for 30 seconds then pour into the ginger chutney mixture and mix well. Set aside.

the chicken

Now place each breast of chicken on a large piece of cling film and flatten them with a meat mallet.

Mix the minced chicken breast with the spring onion, ginger, garam masala and a little salt - and divide into four portions.

Place one portion of mince on flattened chicken breast, roll into a roulade with the cling film. Tighten the ends of cling film by twisting and tying a knot on each end.

Bring the chicken stock to a simmer in a saucepan and poach the roulades for 25-30 minutes or until the chicken is completely cooked through.

Remove roulades from the stock and allow to cool down.

Heat a little oil in a frying pan. Remove the cling film from the chicken roulades and sear them on all sides until lightly colored and crisp.

the sauce

While the chicken is poaching, make the sauce.

Heat the oil in a pan, gently fry the cumin seeds and ginger then add the green chilli and chopped onions.

Fry until the onions are caramelised to a golden-brown then add the chilli powder, coriander and turmeric.

Cook for 2-3 minutes then season with salt and add the chopped tomatoes.

When the tomatoes have softened, place the mixture in a food processor and blend to a fine paste, moistened with a little stock if necessary.

Set the sauce aside and keep warm.

SERVING

Cut each chicken roulade into three equal pieces.

Spoon the sauce and chutney on the plate and place three pieces of roulade on top of the sauce.

Garnish with the fried ginger and cress leaves.

4. <u>Ginger and Coconut Chicken</u>

Flavors of southern India provide a pleasant punch to a basic chicken breast. Exotic, but this is a deceptively easy dish you'll be proud to serve to guests. Serves 4.

Preparation	Cooking	Serving
15 mins	40 mins	60 mins

INGREDIENTS

4 boneless, skinless chicken breast halves, (1-1 1/4 pounds total), trimmed

1 tbsp yellow split peas

1 tsp coriander seeds

1-2 dried red chillis, such as Thai, or cayenne

1/4 cup coconut milk

2 tbsp minced fresh ginger

4 medium cloves garlic, minced or chopped

2 tbsp finely chopped fresh cilantro (coriander)

PREPARATION

Toast split peas, coriander seeds and chilies in a small skillet over medium heat.

Shake pan from time to time, until the split peas turn reddish-brown, the coriander becomes fragrant and the chilies blacken slightly, 2 to 3 mins.

Transfer to a plate to cool for 3 to 5 mins.

Grind in a spice grinder, or mortar and pestle, until mixture is finely ground.

Combine coconut milk, ginger, garlic, cilantro, salt and the spice blend in a shallow glass dish.

Add chicken and turn to coat.

Cover the mix and refrigerate for at least 30 minutes, ideally marinate overnight.

SERVING

Preheat broiler. Coat a broiler-pan rack with cooking spray.

Place the chicken (including marinade) on the rack over the broiler pan. Broil chicken 3 to 5 inches from the heat source until it is no longer pink in the center and the juices run clear, 4 to 6 mins per side.

Serve immediately with your choice of rice or noodles.

CW Tips:

Experiment with different cuts of chicken, bone-in or boneless; just adjust the cooking time accordingly. You can also grill the chicken.

5. Tofu with Peanut and Ginger Sauce

Tofu & vegetables get a great lift from ginger with a spicy peanut sauce. Serve with cucumber salad for a low-calorie, nutrient-packed vegetarian supper. Serve 4.

Preparation	Cooking	Serving
15 mins	20 mins	35 mins

INGREDIENTS

sauce

5 tbsp water

4 tbsp smooth natural peanut butter

1 tbsp rice vinegar, or white vinegar

2 tsp soy sauce

2 tsp honey

2 tsp minced ginger

2 cloves garlic, minced or finely chopped

tofu & vegetables

14 oz extra-firm tofu, preferably water-packed

2 teaspoons extra-virgin olive oil

4 cups baby spinach (6 oz)

1 1/2 cups sliced mushrooms (4 oz)

4 scallions, sliced (1 cup)

PREPARATION

sauce

Whisk (or mixer) the water, peanut butter, rice vinegar (or white vinegar).

Add the soy sauce, honey, ginger and garlic.

tofu & vegetables

Drain and rinse the tofu and pat it dry.

Slice the block cross-wise into eight 1/2-inch thick slabs.

Coarsely crumble each slice into smaller, uneven pieces.

Heat oil in large non-stick skillet, over a high heat.

Add tofu, cook in one layer, no stirring, until pieces begin to turn brown on the bottom, about 5 minutes.

Then stir or turn until all sides are golden brown, 5 minutes more.

Add the spinach, mushrooms, scallions and the peanut sauce and continue stirring, until the vegetables are just cooked, 1 to 2 minutes more.

SERVING

Serve with rice or mashed potato.

CW Tips:

For all non-vegetarians - make this dish with leftover pork or other meat cuts, and serve it over whole grain couscous. The sauce is the secret.

Rice vinegar (or rice-wine vinegar) is mild, slightly sweet vinegar made from fermented rice. Find it in the Asian section of supermarkets and specialty stores

6. Gingerbread - With Orange Icing

I had to include a recipe for gingerbread! - This rich gingerbread is exceptionally good. (Try making it as an alternative for Christmas cake).

Preparation	Cooking	Serving
30 mins	100 mins	130 mins

INGREDIENTS

the cake

225g/8oz butter, softened

225g/8oz light muscovado sugar

225g/8oz golden syrup

225g/8oz black treacle

225g/8oz self-raising flour, sifted

225g/8oz wholemeal self-raising flour, sifted

4 tsp ground ginger, 2 tbsp stem ginger (from a jar)

2 free-range eggs, beaten, 300ml/10½fl oz milk

the icing

150g/5oz icing sugar

1 orange, juice and zest

PREPARATION

the cake

Line a 23cm/9in square cake tin at least 4cm/1½in deep with baking parchment.

Preheat the oven to 160C/325F/Gas 3.

Place the butter, sugar, golden syrup and black treacle into a pan and heat gently until the mixture has melted evenly.

Set aside to cool slightly.

Sift flours, ground ginger and stem ginger into large mixing bowl and mix gently.

Pour the cooled butter mixture into the flour.

Add the eggs and milk and beat with a wooden spoon until well combined.

Pour the cake batter into the tin and level the surface with a palette knife or the back of a spoon.

Bake for 50 minutes, or until the cake has risen and is golden-brown and a skewer inserted into the middle comes out clean.

Set aside to cool slightly in the tin, then transfer the cake to a wire rack and set aside to cool completely.

the icing

Meanwhile, for the orange icing, sift the icing sugar into a bowl.

Add 2 tablespoons of the orange juice and mix to a smooth paste.

Add more orange juice, as necessary, until you get a smooth icing of the consistency you desire.

SERVING

Pour the icing over the cooled cake and spread lightly, allowing it to ooze over the edges.

Sprinkle over chopped orange zest and set the cake aside until the icing has set.

Cut and serve.

CW Tips:

Have the neighbors around for coffee and gingerbread!

7. Ginger Cup Cakes

Ginger gives these cup cakes a lovely little kick, even if you don't like pumpkin that much. These will disappear fast so watch out! Serves – 12 (2 each!)

Preparation	Cooking	Serving
20 mins	20 mins	50 mins

INGREDIENTS

2 cups all-purpose flour

1 (3.4oz) package instant butterscotch pudding mix

2 teaspoons baking soda

1/4 tsp salt, 1 tbsp ground cinnamon

1/2 tsp ground ginger

1/2 tsp ground allspice

1/4 tsp ground cloves

1/3 cup finely chopped ginger

1 cup butter, at room temperature

1 cup white sugar

1 cup packed brown sugar, 4 eggs

1 tsp vanilla extract

1 can pumpkin puree (15 oz)

PREPARATION

Grease 24 muffin cups, or line with paper muffin liners.

Whisk together the flour, pudding mix, baking soda, salt, cinnamon, ground ginger, allspice, cloves, and crystallized ginger in a bowl; set aside.

Beat the butter, white sugar, and brown sugar with an electric mixer in a large bowl until light and fluffy.

The mixture should be noticeably lighter in color.

Add the room-temperature eggs one at a time, allowing each egg to blend into the butter mixture before adding the next.

Beat in the vanilla and pumpkin puree with the last egg.

Stir in the flour mixture, mixing until just incorporated.

Pour the batter into the prepared muffin cups.

Bake in preheated oven 175°C/350°F until golden and the tops spring back when lightly pressed, about 20 minutes.

Cool for 10 mins then place on a wire rack.

8. Soft Ginger Cookies

The perfect coffee break snack – these big cookies are soft and chewy, gingerbread cookies. They stay soft to last a few snack times. Serves – 24.

Preparation	Cooking	Serving
15 mins	10 mins	45 mins

INGREDIENTS

2 1/4 cups all-purpose flour

2 tsp ground ginger

1 tsp baking soda, 3/4 tsp ground cinnamon

1/2 tsp ground cloves

1/4 tsp salt

3/4 cup margarine, softened

1 cup white sugar

1 egg, 1 tbsp water

1/4 cup molasses, 2 tbsp white sugar

PREPARATION

Sift together the flour, ginger, baking soda, cinnamon, cloves, and salt.

In a large bowl, cream together the margarine and 1 cup sugar until light and fluffy.

Beat in the egg, then stir in the water and molasses.

Gradually stir the sifted ingredients into the molasses mixture.

Shape the dough into walnut sized balls

Roll them in the remaining 2 tablespoons of sugar.

Place the cookies 2 inches apart onto an ungreased cookie sheet, and flatten slightly.

Bake for 8 to 10 minutes in a preheated oven at 175°C/350°F.

SERVING

Allow cookies to cool on baking sheet for 5 minutes

Place on a wire rack to cool completely.

Serve or store in an airtight container.

9. <u>Ginger Marmalade</u>

The best ginger marmalade that I have tasted. I found this recipe in an old cookery book and it is the business for a fresh start on my toast!

Preparation	Cooking	Serving
25 mins	20 mins	480 mins

INGREDIENTS

3 1/2 cups peeled fresh ginger

4 cups water

5 cups white sugar

1 (3 oz) pouch of liquid pectin

5 half pint canning jars with lids and rings

PREPARATION

Divide the ginger in half, and chop one half into cubes.

Shred the other half with a box grater or in a food processor.

Place the ginger into a large saucepan with water over medium heat

Bring to a boil, cover, and simmer until ginger is tender (approx 75 mins). Add more water if needed to keep mixture from drying out.

Pour the cooked ginger into a fine-mesh strainer, drain, and retain 1/2 cup of the ginger-flavored water.

Place the cooked ginger in a bowl with the retained liquid, and cool at least 4 hours (or overnight) in refrigerator.

When ginger is thoroughly cooled, place into a large, heavy-bottomed pot, and stir in the sugar.

Bring to a boil over medium-high heat, and boil hard for 1 minute, stirring constantly.

Stir in the pouch of liquid pectin, reduce heat and simmer for 7 more minutes, skimming foam from top of marmalade.

Sterilize the canning jars and lids in boiling water for at least 5 minutes.

Pack the marmalade into the hot, sterilized jars, filling the jars to within 1/4 inch of the top.

Run a knife or a thin spatula around the insides of the jars after they have been filled to remove any air bubbles.

Wipe the rims of the jars with a moist paper towel to remove any food residue.

Top the jars with lids, and screw on rings.

Place a rack in the bottom of a large stockpot and fill halfway with water.

Bring to a boil over high heat, then carefully lower the jars into the pot using a holder.

Leave a 2 inch space between the jars.

Pour in more boiling water if necessary until the water level is at least 1 inch above the tops of the jars.

Bring the water to a full boil, cover the pot, and process for 15 minutes.

Remove the jars from the stockpot and place onto a cloth-covered or wood surface, several inches apart, until cool.

Once cooled, press the top of each lid with a finger, ensuring that the seal is tight (lid does not move up or down at all).

Store in a cool, dark place.

CW Tips:

This ginger marmalade is great on top of toast, but can also be used as a glaze for ham or chicken, substituted for any jam in baking, or as a dip for lamb instead of mint jelly.

10. Homemade Ginger Tea

Real ginger tea has a spicy, invigorating taste. Prepare and use as a home remedy for indigestion, nausea, and to ward off colds, flu and sore throats.

Preparation	Cooking	Serving
5 mins	15-20 mins	25 mins

INGREDIENTS

4 cups of water

2-inch piece of fresh ginger root (fresh is best for tea)

Optional: honey and lemon slice (great additions for healthy kick)

PREPARATION

Peel the ginger root and slice it into thin slices.

Bring the water to a boil in a saucepan. Once it is boiling, add the ginger.

Cover it and reduce to a simmer for 15-20 minutes. Strain the tea. Add honey and lemon to taste.

2 - Introduction to Chives

Section 2 is dedicated to one of the most popular herbs which can be used as an accompaniment for almost any dish – chives.

This is a delightfully tasty herb that belongs to the onion family, and is known botanically as *allium schoenoprasium*, derived from the Greek meaning 'reed-like leek'

The genus *allium* has in fact about 500 species - other common plants in this genus are onions, garlic, scallions and even leeks.

Valued for their flavor, the smallest member of the onion family has many wild cousins growing throughout the Northern hemisphere.

Chives are perennials (grow every year) and will grow in most garden soils. Unlike some herbs, they actually thrive in the full sun. While many people know that the green straw-like leaves are edible, the flowers - pink or lavender in color - are also edible.

Marco Polo is reputed to have experienced chives on his travels in China, where they were a native plant, and reported on their culinary attributes on his return to the West, where they were readily accepted and have been cultivated ever since.

The Uses of Chives

Chives' leaves have a fairly strong onion flavor and they are used in a variety of dishes – often together with eggs and potatoes. They are also great in salads, soups and stews - but if they are to be used in cooked dishes they should be introduced at the last moment to best preserve their flavour.

Chives are easy to grow, have a long season and are of course better used fresh than dried. They can be successfully frozen and stored for use in winter.

Chives grow in clumps like grass, sending up graceful, hollow, thin leaves up to 12 inches. Unlike regular onions however, no large bulb forms underground, and it is the leaves that are the strong source of onion flavor.

As a perennial plant **chives** are perfect for home gardening, for experts and for beginners. If you grow your own chives, you will be blessed in the spring and summer with lovely lavender flowers shaped like a delicate puffball (see image).

As mentioned, these flowers are also edible, and make a strikingly colorful garnish for any dish. The leaves are grass-like and lovely in mashed potatoes, sauces and salads.

Be aware that the flavor of chives becomes harsher after flowering. If you want to prevent chives from flowering, simply keep snipping the leaves back.

One variety, garlic **chives**, are great for times when you have run out of garlic and need to whip up a meal that requires garlic.

Simply chop up the 'bulb' end of the plant for most flavor.

Also known as Chinese chives, garlic chives (allium tuberosum), can be used and stored in the same manner as chives.

Garlic Chives are distinguished by their flat, broad leaves and fragrant white flowers. Otherwise, they look very similar in appearance.

As you would expect, garlic chives have a delicate garlic flavor and are used extensively in oriental dishes.

They are a good choice for those who shy away from full-flavored garlic, just as regular chives are happily consumed by those who do not care for the strong taste of fresh onions or scallions.

Ordinary **chives** generally have a mild taste and are rather juicy. Fresh chives add flavor, heat and spice to a great variety of dishes.

A mention of **chives** brings to mind a baked potato with all the trimmings, but there is so much more to this thin, graceful herb.

Chives are easy to grow indoors and out, and are also available freeze-dried, making them the perfect year-round herb to have to hand.

And to whet your appetite and get you busy enjoying chives - I have selected 10 of my favourite recipes which use chives as a key ingredient.

Chives as Medicine

Chives have medicinal value similar to that of garlic - and have long been used in Chinese medicine for colds, flu, and lung congestion.

They are less used medicinally in the west, but are still helpful. Mildly antibiotic, they can stimulate a poor appetite, and chive leaves are also useful as they are mildly laxative.

Chives can also be used as part of a diet, with the leaves chewed slowly or minced and sprinkled on food to lower blood pressure, reduce cholesterol and to prevent miscarriage - as well as for anemia, bleeding, internal mucous, tuberculosis, urinary problems, and general debility.

The **chives** genus can help to fight germs, prevent heart attacks and arthritis, fight tumors and lower blood sugar.

A National Cancer Institute study reported that eating allium vegetables lowered the risk of men developing prostate cancer.

A similar French study noted that while allium vegetables may lower the risk of stomach and colorectal cancers, further research is needed to be conclusive about this.

Chives, chopped and sprinkled on food, will definitely aid digestion and stimulate poor appetite.

Today, Chinese cooks put garlic chives' antiseptic qualities to good use by combining the chives with pork fat to season a wok.

Growing Chives at Home

You can grow **chives** to complement your landscape and to keep insects away from your most treasured bulbs - chives will in particular help to prevent aphids – those little herbivorous insects that are more commonly known as plant lice, without having to use harmful pesticides.

Chives are usually bought as small plants, but they also can also be easily grown from seeds. If you already have a clump of chives, you can increase the crop easily by simply dividing the roots.

Chives do best in moist, fairly rich soil and in full sun. Common chives are evergreen (or nearly so) in mild regions, and go dormant where winters are severe.

Chinese **chives** are less energetic than common chives and more inclined to be dormant in winter.

A sheltered, moist spot in a warm climate will provide enough humidity. If you have problems with dry air then regular spraying and misting might help.

The plant is pretty enough to use as an edging for flower borders or an herb garden, and the flowers even can be cut and used in arrangements.

In summary then:

Chives Like:

A rich moist soil

Good sunlight

Warm weather

Shade in long hot summers

Chives Dislike:

Frost

Soggy, waterlogged soil

Strong winds

Growing Chives in a Container

1. Chives are ideally suited to container culture and will grow happily in just a potting compost (but do add some organic fertilizer to encourage healthy growth).

2. Chives actually demand little attention throughout the year, just be sure to water if the compost is drying out.

3. Use a pot or container that's about a foot across and a foot deep, and has good drainage at the bottom (pinch a few holes in base if necessary).

4. Feed your plants with a monthly small dose of fertilizer throughout the growing season. You may wish to consider using "compost tea" or "manure tea" as an organic fertilizer.

5. If the container remains outside, take your chives indoors in the fall, or at least close to the house walls, as they're less tolerant of cold temperatures when grown in pots. This way you get to enjoy chives through the winter.

6. Clip the young, tender stems any time, and use for garnishing.

Growing Chives in the Garden

1. If you live in a colder climate - start your chives indoors, it may be too cold outside in spring for instance. (See Container Tips).

2. If growing chives from seed, sow the seeds in the spring in a sunlit place and cover with a light compost or seed starter. Be sure to keep the soil warm and moist until you see the growing seedlings appear (normally within 7 days).

3. Chives grow best in bunches, so thin your plants to approximately 6 plants per bunch, leaving at least 1 foot of space between bunches.

4. When the seedlings are ready to be planted outside in the garden – choose a soil that is well dug up and bolstered with organic compost. Water only when the soil has dried out. If your garden has good soil the added compost should be good enough. If your soil is too heavy consider a raised bed, or a small ridge to improve drainage. The soil should not dry out.

5. Be careful not to overwater though, because the water that drains away will take vital nutrients with it.

6. Be sure to keep the soil weed free to let the chives get established. It is a good idea to mulch the ground after planting to keep down weeds.

7. If the soil has been prepared as described above, just sit back and watch the plants grow - they are almost completely free of disease, and their only requirement is watering if the conditions become very dry.

8. They may occasionally suffer from onion fly, but this is almost always because they have been planted near onions which have been attacked - the solution is not to plant chives near onions!

9. Chives are perennial plants, and keep their leaves in most winters. In colder winters, the leaves may die back completely, but don't despair - their roots are still alive and they will begin new growth next spring.

Chives Harvesting Tips

1. Chives usually grow to approximately 45 centimetres (18 inches) in height with a beautiful round purple flower.

2. If you don't intend to eat the chive flowers or harvest the seeds, then you should remove the flower buds as soon as possible. Chive flowers, if left on your plants, will slow the growing of new leaves, as most of the plant's energy instead goes into producing the flowers.

3. If you've planted chives by seeds, do not harvest until late in the growing season in the first year. Otherwise, plan to cut the leaves regularly. This ensures a continual supply of tender leaves.

4. When the flowers start dying back, you can cut the plant down. Cut the leaves with scissors, starting at the outside of the plant and working your way to the center. Leave approximately 2 to 3 inches of leaves remaining on the plant.

5. The leaves rapidly grow back and can be cut several times in the growing season. Plants grown from seed should be left alone (although remove the emerging flower heads) until July in the first year to allow a good root system to establish itself.

6. Whilst chives are best used fresh, they can be stored too. You could dry the flower stalks by hanging it upside down or on racks in a warm, airy and dry place. Alternatively, you could freeze the chopped chives.

7. After 3 to 4 years, the plant should be divided into smaller bunches and replanted. After gently digging the plant up, separate the clumps of bulbs and plant back into fertile soil. If your chives die during winter, do not worry, as they will come back in spring.

8. Chives produce flowers in spring, and a second flush may well occur between June to July. If you are growing the plants for eating alone, these flowers should be removed as soon as possible.

9. If the flowers are required for eating or for their color, it is best to keep a couple of chive plants expressly for this purpose.

10. The bulbs of chives are edible as mild onions. As mentioned the flowers are definitely edible and are great added to salads - their color makes salads come alive. The flower heads are actually a mass of smaller flowers, which should be separated before adding to the salad. The stalk is also edible, but is quite tasteless and tough - throw it away!

11. Freezing your own chives is a great way of ensuring an always available food ingredient – but with the flavor of fresh spice. For freezing, the leaves should be snipped off about 2" above ground and the remaining part closest to the ground snipped into small lengths and frozen in single layers.

12. Don't wash them yet – you do that just before using them in the recipe, but it might be an idea to discard the really grotty bits.

.. and finally (chives)

A simple sprinkling of chopped chives livens up the appearance of a bowl of soup, or tops off a fresh salad perfectly.

Chives similar to onions, have a bulbous but small root. The bulbs multiply quickly over a few years and this provides the easiest method of propagation.

Simply dig up the clump of bulbs in March or October, carefully separate them into individual bulbs and replant with the tips of the bulbs level with the soil surface.

They thrive on this method of propagation, because it relieves the congestion in the bulbs.

Now for some tasty recipes..

My Top 10 Recipes with Chives

There are several new varieties of chives available from specialist seed merchants and they aim to provide plants which produce very fine leaves, much preferred by cooks. I have tried some of these and they do indeed produce finer leaves, but only in the first year.

The seeds are cheap, so try a few varieties, but I still recommend the common chive for most purposes.

Chives should be used fresh, otherwise they lose almost all their flavor. When used with cooked foods, add them after cooking. They can be dried, but again there is little point because they then have little flavor.

One way to store them is to chop the leaves into 1cm (half inch) lengths and place them in ice cube containers with some water. Freeze them, and then defrost an ice cube or two when need to use them.

11.   Prawn and Avocado with Chives

A lovely flavorsome and healthy dish, best with raw prawns but can be good with frozen prawns too.

Preparation	Cooking	Serving
15 mins	15 mins	30 mins

INGREDIENTS

300g raw or thawed prawns

2 cloves garlic

2 fresh avocados

1 lettuce

For the dressing:

1/3 cup fresh chives

½ cup fresh parsley

50g anchovies

½ cup cream

2 tbsp apple vinegar

1 tsp Dijon mustard

1 tsp Worcestershire/Soy sauce

1 tbsp lemon juice

½ cup cream (or alternative)

1 cup mayonnaise, pepper (freshly ground) to taste

PREPARATION

Sauté the prawns in butter and add crushed fresh garlic. Set aside.

Peel and cut avocado into quarters.

Find a suitable salad bowl and toss the prawns with the lettuce (washed, dried and shredded).

Refrigerate.

For the dressing:

Chop the chives and parsley, and mince the anchovies.

Combine, then refrigerate until required.

SERVING

Add the avocado pieces, and toss with half the prepared dressing.

12.   Steak Diane

A stunning 'restaurant' dish you can easily make at home. Tender filet mignon steaks with a rich cream sauce - perfect for a romantic dinner.

Preparation	Cooking	Serving
10 mins	6 mins	20 mins

INGREDIENTS

4 (3 oz each) center cut beef tenderloin medallions, trimmed of all fat and pounded to 1/2 inch thick, chilled

1 oz butter

1 tsp Worcestershire sauce

2 tablespoons shallots, chopped

1/8 tsp garlic, minced

1/4 cup mushroom caps, sliced 1/8 inch thick

1 tbsp lemon juice, freshly squeezed

1 tsp dry mustard powder

1/2 tsp thyme leaves, fresh if possible

2 oz fresh cream

1 oz brandy

1 tbsp parsley, chopped

1 tbsp chives, chopped

Salt, pepper, freshly ground, to taste

PREPARATION

n a small 8-10 inch sauté pan, heat 1 tbsp butter over medium heat for 1 minute.

Add the tenderloin steaks, sprinkle with a little salt and pepper, increase heat to medium-high and sauté exactly 2 minutes on each side.

Remove them to a plate and chill in a refrigerator for 5 minutes.

Preheat a large (12-inch) sauté pan over medium heat for 1 minute.

Add clarified butter, then add the Worcestershire sauce to the butter.

Place the shallots, garlic, and mushrooms in the center of the pan with the tenderloin steaks around the edges.

With a spoon, stir and toss the mushroom mixture.

After 2 minutes add the lemon juice and season the ingredients with salt and fresh ground black pepper.

Turn filet steaks and add the thyme, chopped parsley and dried mustard powder.

Cook the steaks as you like them.

Leave in the pan and add the cream and chives.

Tilt the pan slightly, and pour the brandy into the front edge of the pan, turn the heat to high and let the flame (or if electric, light with a match) catch the brandy's vapors and ignite it.

Swirl slightly, turn off the heat and let the flame go out.

SERVING

Place filet mignon medallions on plates and top with the sauce from the pan.

Serve immediately with choice of rice.

CW Tips:

You may want to slightly undercook the filet mignon steaks prior to adding the cream and brandy so that the reduction process of making the sauce doesn't overcook them.

13. Crab Muffins with Chives

Little seafood muffins are bursting with flavor. Crab muffin appetizers may be served warm or at room temperature for a perfect party finger food.

Preparation	Cooking	Serving
30 mins	30 mins	60 mins

INGREDIENTS

Vegetable spray:

1/4 cup (1/2 stick) butter

1/4 cup minced sweet onions

1/4 cup minced celery

2 cloves garlic, pressed

1-1/2 cups strong fish, chicken, or vegetable broth

1 (6 ounces) box stuffing mix

1 cup shredded Swiss cheese

2 cups fresh crabmeat, or pasteurized canned lump crabmeat

2 tbsp chopped chives

3 medium eggs

1/4 cup lemon juice

PREPARATION

Sauté sweet onions and celery in butter until onion becomes translucent.

Add pressed garlic and sauté an additional 2 minutes.

Add broth and bring to a boil. Remove from heat.

Add contents of stuffing mix, gently tossing to combine.

Let rest, uncovered, for 15 minutes.

Preheat oven to 175°C/350°F. Coat mini-muffin tins with vegetable spray.

Toss Swiss cheese, crabmeat, and chives with prepared stuffing mix.

Beat eggs, lemon juice, and milk with a fork until mixed.

Let sit for 5 minutes until it appears curdled.

Pour egg mixture over crab stuffing mix. Toss gently to combine.

Fill mini-muffin tins to the rim.

Bake about 30 minutes until puffy and golden.

SERVING

Serve hot or at room temperature with optional dipping sauce.

CW Tips:

Try substituting lobster, smoked salmon, or tuna for the crab meat.

14.   American Shepherd's Pie

American variation of traditional English shepherd's pie with beef - that is sure to please any meat and potatoes fan.

Preparation	Cooking	Serving
20 mins	40 mins	60 mins

INGREDIENTS

1 tbsp olive oil

1 pound ground chuck (minced) beef

6 oz mushrooms, chopped

1-2 chopped onions, to taste

2 large cloves garlic, pressed or chopped

1 tbsp soy sauce

1 tbsp flour

1/2 cup beef broth, 1/2 cup frozen peas

2 cups shredded hash brown potatoes (frozen or deli-packed)

1/2 cup chopped chives

2 cups finely-shredded Cheddar cheese

A pinch of paprika, or chilli powder

PREPARATION

Preheat oven to 190°C/375°F. Heat oil in a pan, add chives, beef, mushrooms, onion, garlic, salt and pepper.

Sauté, breaking up ground beef, until the juices have almost evaporated.

Stir in soy sauce, then flour. Cook for 1 minute, stirring.

Add beef broth, stirring to combine, and simmer until gravy thickens.

Pour into baking dish, cool slightly, then sprinkle green peas on top.

In a mixing bowl, combine hash brown potatoes, chives, 1 cup of cheese, salt. Spread evenly on top of dish.

Sprinkle remaining cheese on top and a pinch of paprika.

Bake for about 40 minutes in the oven, cheese will be nice and crispy.

CW Tips:

For more authentic shepherd's pie, use lamb instead of beef.

15.   Stuffed Potatoes with Chives

An alternative potato dish, really tasty accompaniment to a cold meat lunch.

Preparation	Cooking	Serving
15 mins	20 mins	35 mins

INGREDIENTS

4 large baking potatoes

2 tbsp (30ml) olive oil

1 leek, sliced

175g button mushrooms, sliced

3 tbsp (45ml) milk

4 tsp (20ml) horseradish sauce

1 egg, beaten

2 tbsp (30ml) fresh chives, chopped

100g Gruyere cheese, grated

PREPARATION

the sauce

Preheat the oven to 190°C/375°F.

Heat one tbsp (15ml) of the oil in a frying pan and cook the leeks and mushrooms for 5 minutes until softened.

Remove the potatoes from the oven. Allow them to cool and then cut in half lengthways.

Scoop the potato flesh into a bowl leaving the skins intact.

Mash the potatoes and stir in the remaining olive oil, cooked leeks and mushrooms, milk, horseradish sauce, egg, chives, half the cheese and seasoning.

Pile mixture back into the skins, sprinkle with the remaining cheese and bake for about 5 to 8 minutes until they look tasty.

SERVING

Serve with cold meat or smoked salmon.

16. Zucchini Pate

Try this 'no-cook' pate to serve as a dip or spread with herb crackers or raw sliced vegetable bites.

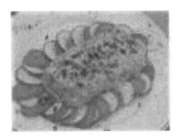

Preparation	Cooking	Serving
25 mins	0 mins	25 mins

INGREDIENTS

2 tsp white wine vinegar

1 tsp sugar; 1 tsp salt, divided use

1 medium zucchini (about 1/4 pound), unpeeled and coarsely grated

1/4 cup minced sweet onion

1/4 cup packed fresh parsley sprigs

1/2 cup chopped fresh chives

1 (3 oz) cream cheese, at room temperature

1/4 tsp ground white pepper

1/4 cup roasted red pepper, coarsely chopped

PREPARATION

Place wine vinegar, sugar, and 1/2 tsp salt in a zip-top bag.

Seal and squish to combine.

Add grated zucchini and minced sweet onion, seal and toss to coat.

Re-open, squeeze out all the air, and seal again.

Let sit for 1 hour to release the excess water.

Line a colander or bowl with cheesecloth.

Pour zucchini into colander, bring up the corners of the cheesecloth, and twist to squeeze out as much moisture as possible.

Transfer zucchini and onions to a food processor fitted with the metal blade. Add parsley and chives, process until smooth.

Add cream cheese, 1/2 tsp salt, and pepper. Process until combined.

Add roasted red peppers and pulse until peppers are reduced to small flecks.

Scrape zucchini pate into a small mold lined with plastic wrap or a small bowl.

Cover with plastic wrap pressed to the surface and refrigerate 4 hours/overnight.

SERVING

To unmold, remove top plastic wrap.

Invert mold or bowl over a decorative plate.

Remove the bottom layer of plastic wrap. Serve with herb crackers, or carrot sticks.

17. <u>Chicken Stuffed with Chives</u>

Chicken breasts stuffed with a garlic, chives, and cream cheese mixture, wrapped with a slice of bacon, and topped with butter.

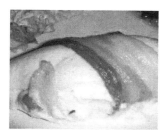

Preparation	Cooking	Serving
15 mins	30 mins	45 mins

INGREDIENTS

1 (8 oz) cream cheese, softened

2 tbsp dried chives, better still freshly chopped from the garden

1 clove garlic, chopped or pressed

4 skinless, boneless chicken breast halves

4 slices of bacon

2 tbsp butter, melted

PREPARATION

Preheat oven to 175°C/350°F.

In a bowl, mix the cream cheese, chives, and garlic.

Divide the mixture into 4 balls.

Place 1 cream cheese ball in the center of each chicken breast half.

Fold the chicken over the cream cheese, wrap with a slice of turkey bacon, and secure with toothpicks.

Arrange the chicken in a baking dish.

Pour the butter over the chicken.

Bake 30 minutes in the preheated oven, or until the bacon is crisp and the chicken is no longer pink and juices run clear.

SERVING

Serve with potatoes of your choice, I prefer mashed.

18. Potato Soup with Chives

A really tasty and nourishing soup perfect for lunchtime or as a starter.

Preparation	Cooking	Serving
15 mins	30 mins	45 mins

INGREDIENTS

4 large potatoes, peeled and sliced

4 cups chicken stock

1 large clove garlic

1 cup shredded Cheddar cheese, or similar

1/2 cup chopped fresh chives

Salt and freshly ground black pepper

1 cup cream, half-and-half, or soured cream (optional)

1/4 cup crumbled Cheddar cheese, for garnish

PREPARATION

Place the potatoes and 1 cup of stock in the slow cooker.

Cover and cook on high for 2 hours, or until the potatoes are just tender.

Transfer two-thirds of the potatoes to a food processor or blender, along with the cooking liquid.

Add the garlic. Blend to the desired consistency (a blender will yield a smooth texture, a food processor a rough, rustic consistency).

Return the potato purée to the slow cooker and stir in the shredded cheese, the remaining 2/3 cup stock, and the chives.

Cover and cook on low for 30 minutes, or until the soup is well heated.

Add extra stock or water if the soup is too thick. Break up the whole potato slices with a fork to achieve a texture that suits you.

Season.

SERVING

Serve with a good dollop of soured cream and sprinkle with plenty of chives.

CW Tips:

If you don't have a slow cooker amend times to suit cooking normally.

19.   <u>Chilli with Chive Potatoes</u>

A great way to vary your chilli incorporating chives and potatoes in a really flavorsome and simple dish.

Preparation	Cooking	Serving
15 mins	25 mins	40 mins

INGREDIENTS

450g pack reduced-fat pork sausages

2 tsp vegetable oil

1kg new potatoes , skins on, thickly sliced

2 red peppers sliced

2 garlic cloves, chopped or crushed

1 tsp each ground coriander, chilli powder and cumin

400g can red kidney beans in water, rinsed and drained

2 x 400g cans chopped tomatoes (ideally with herbs)

2 tsp caster sugar

5 tbsp low fat Greek yogurt

20g pack chives, snipped

PREPARATION

Squeeze 3 balls of meat from each sausage, fry in the oil for 5 mins until golden.

While they cook, put the potatoes on to boil for 10 mins until tender.

Add the peppers to the pan, then fry for 4 mins more.

Tip in the garlic and spices, fry for 1 min, then add the beans, tomatoes and sugar.

Simmer for 5 mins until saucy and the meatballs are cooked.

Drain the potatoes, then crush with a masher.

Fold through the yogurt and chives, loosen with a splash of water.

SERVING

Equally good served immediately, or allowed to cool for heating later.

Serve mash or rice with the chilli.

Top with a dollop more yogurt and sprinkling of fresh chives.

20.   <u>Chives Omelet</u>

Left with a bunch of chives in your fridge? – a great way to use them up while still fresh, a simple recipe which is fast to prepare.

Preparation	Cooking	Serving
5 mins	15-20 mins	25 mins

INGREDIENTS

3 oz chives (any kind)

4 large eggs

1 tbsp oil

Seasonings:

1/8 tsp sesame oil

1/2 tsp fish sauce

1/2 tsp oyster sauce, a pinch of salt and pepper

PREPARATION

Cut the chives into small pieces. Set aside.

Beat the eggs and then season with all the ingredients for Seasonings.

Add the chives to the eggs.

Heat up the oil in a wok or skillet over high heat.

Pour the eggs into the wok or skillet, swirl the eggs around so they coat the wok or skillet evenly.

As soon as the sides start to cook, flip the eggs over.

Continue to cook until the eggs turn light brown or set.

Top off with grated cheese.

SERVING

Dish out and serve immediately.

CW Tips:

Add other leftover ingredients, like tomatoes or mushrooms.

3 - Introduction To Garlic

Section 3 is dedicated to the incredible and wonderfully 'aromatic' herb we know as **garlic**.

Garlic is a part of the *allium genus - allium sativum* in fact - and thus forms part of the onion family. It is, of course, best known as a fantastic cooking ingredient, used for its wonderful taste worldwide.

The genus allium has in fact about 500 species - other common plants in this genus are onions, chives, scallions and even leeks.

Garlic is actually considered both a vegetable and an herb. It has been used medicinally for thousands of years - since ancient Greek and Roman times.

For the last 4000 years of human history **garlic** has been both cherished and reviled, both sought after for its healing powers, and shunned for its pungent after effects!

From miracle drug then to 'vampire repellent' to offerings for the gods, this extraordinary plant has had an undeniably important place in human history, and today enjoys a renewed surge in popularity as modern medicine unearths the wonders of this ancient superfood.

The psychological term for fear of garlic is alliumphobia.

Garlic is an excellent garden choice for even the newest of gardeners - as it is simple to grow, tastes delicious, and keeps well.

Garlic grows well in almost all climates, and the bulbs from one harvest can be used the following year.

Individual cloves act as seeds. The bulbs grow underground and the leaves shoot in to the air.

Although **garlic** is traditionally thought of as a Mediterranean plant - it is also grown successfully in colder Northern climates. The majority of garlic grown in the USA comes from California.

There are many different **garlic** varieties, the two most common varieties being the common 'hardneck' (stronger flavor) and the 'softneck' (wild garlic).

Garlic's uniquely pungent flavor is due to a chemical reaction that occurs when the garlic cells are broken. The flavor is most intense just after mincing.

The smell of **garlic** can be actually be removed by running your hands under cold water while rubbing a stainless steel object.

When picking out garlic at the grocery store, choose firm, tight, heavy dry bulbs.

It is also commonly believed that **garlic** will improve your sexual health. The potency of garlic as an aphrodisiac was confirmed by Aristotle and in ancient Indian writings

The Uses of Garlic

Fresh **garlic** has many active constituents including allicin, alliinase and unique sulfur compounds.

Allicin and the sulfur compounds are the ingredients primarily responsible for garlic's potency as an antibiotic, anti-viral and a fungicide, and also for its use in treating high blood pressure, lowering cholesterol, and helping to prevent certain types of cancer, as well as its use as an immune stimulant.

Garlic has also been used to treat acne, warts, and toothaches. Even if your garlic has sprouted, it is still usable although it has lost some of its flavor and health benefits.

If your rose garden is being attacked by aphids, an excellent home remedy to get rid of them is to spray the leaves and blooms with a mixture of crushed garlic and water.

You can use **garlic** to repel night-time mosquitoes by placing cloves where there are mosquitoes, or by applying extracts on exposed parts of your skin.

Simply mix **garlic** cloves and extracts with pepper and a bit of soap to make your own garlic pesticide. Some gardeners even use garlic mixtures to keep animals such as rabbits, deer, and groundhogs away from their vegetables.

If you don't have a bottle of adhesive or glue in your house, you can use a bunch of **garlic** cloves to make instant glue. Take the cloves out and crush them - the glue can be made by rubbing garlic juices on paper or glass!

And **garlic** has blood cleansing and antibiotic properties that can be effective against acne and other skin ailments. Some people say that you can get rid of persistent pimples by rubbing raw garlic cloves on your face. You may also crush garlic cloves and extract their juices to use.

And if you're going out on a date, consider putting a little garlic on the menu, just enough to keep the passion flowing without the odor getting in the way.

To whet your appetite and get you busy enjoying garlic - I have selected 10 more of my favourite recipes which use garlic as a key ingredient.

These feature at the end of the book.

Garlic as Medicine

As already, various garlic health benefits have long been claimed and the "stinking rose" treatment has been used extensively in herbal medicine (*phytotherapy*) down the centuries.

It has been considered by many to be a herbal "wonder drug", with a reputation in folklore for preventing or treating everything from the common cold and flu to the Plague!

Amongst the most interesting potential applications are suggestions that garlic might be able to assist in the management of blood pressure and cholesterol levels.

The key is *allicin*, which is broken down into the foul-smelling sulphur compounds which taint breath.

These compounds react with red blood cells and produce hydrogen sulphide which relaxes the blood vessels, and keeps blood flowing easily.

Garlic is widely believed to ward off colds, and flu. The consumption of garlic as well as lowering blood cholesterol levels will reduce the build-up of plaque in the arteries, and help prevent heart disease.

Modern science has shown that **garlic** is a powerful natural antibiotic, albeit broad-spectrum rather than targeted. The bacteria in the body do not appear to evolve resistance to the garlic as they do to many modern pharmaceutical antibiotics.

This means that garlic's positive health benefits can continue over time rather than helping to breed antibiotic resistant "superbugs".

Studies have also shown that **garlic** - can have a powerful antioxidant effect. Antioxidants can help to protect the body against damaging free radicals.

Some people who want to benefit from the health benefits without the taste prefer to take **garlic** supplements. These pills and capsules have the advantage of avoiding garlic breath.

Research suggests that people who take a garlic supplement each day are less likely to fall victim to the common cold.

It is important to note that large amounts in supplement form may interact with blood thinning drugs and could increase the risk of bleeding.

Raw **garlic** is very strong, so eating too much could digestive problems. There are also some people who are allergic to garlic. Symptoms of garlic allergy include skin rash, temperature and headaches.

It also found that allicin-containing garlic supplements were effective in treating infections caused by the hospital superbug, MRSA. Plants do not have an immune system - they fight viruses and infections with in-built chemical defences.

So, if you like, allicin is one of the chemical defences of **garlic** which helps keep it healthy. In this study we are simply using the plant's natural defence to fight our own virus.

A National Cancer Institute study reported that eating *allium* vegetables lowered the risk of men developing prostate cancer. A similar French study noted that while allium vegetables may lower the risk of stomach and colorectal cancers, further research is needed to be conclusive about this.

Growing Garlic at Home

To grow **garlic** you need to choose a garden site that gets plenty of sun and where the soil is not too damp. Unlike some herbs, garlic can thrive in the full sun.

Plant the cloves individually, upright and about an inch (25 mm) under the surface, plant the cloves about 4 inches (100 mm) apart with rows about 18 inches (450 mm) apart.

When it comes to cooking there's really no substitute for the original stinking rose. A sheltered, moist spot in a warm climate will provide enough humidity. If you have problems with dry air then regular spraying and misting might help.

The softneck (wild garlic) variety stores longer but the hardneck variety has a stronger flavor.

If you have the room, grow some of each type.

Be a little wary of planting garlic purchased at the greengrocers, as this is likely to be imported garlic - with an associated risk of introducing virus diseases to your soil.

Garlic Likes:

A loose fertile soil

Good sunlight

Plenty of fertile compost

Garlic Dislikes:

Competition from weeds

Dry soil, especially when bulbing

Growing near peas or beans

Growing Garlic in a Container

1. The best time to plant garlic in containers is mid-October but up to mid-April is fine. Because you will be using potting compost in the pots, the cloves can be bought from your local supermarket.

2. Fill a 20 cm (8 inch) pot - with a similar depth to allow for good root growth - with normal potting compost (don't use soil from the garden).

3. Gently remove the outer skin from the bulb (not the cloves) and separate into individual cloves.

4. Plant one clove per pot in an upright position 2cm (1in) below the soil surface.

5. Ensure the pot has good drainage at the bottom (pinch a few holes in base if necessary).

6. Feed your plants with a regular but small dose of fertilizer throughout the growing season. You may wish to consider using "compost tea" or "manure tea" as an organic fertilizer, or worm juice (my favorite).

7. Water the container well and place in a sunny position. If you are planting in October, then place the pots out of the way of cold winds. By the edge of the house where they still get the sun is ideal, like most plants they are less tolerant of cold temperatures when grown in pots.

8. Garlic will flourish when grown in a container. The soil should be kept well-drained and they can be fed easily. The problem is the fact that they are not particularly attractive plants.

Growing Garlic in the Garden

1. Break the bulbs into individual cloves ready for planting. Select the largest eight or so of the cloves which will be on the outside of the bulb. Take care not to damage the cloves as this can lead to rotting.

2. In colder regions plant the cloves in divided seed trays of multi-purpose compost. Plant the pointy end up. Water well and place trays in a cool greenhouse or cold frame to grow on.

3. Garlic plants grown in trays will be ready to plant out in March or April. Use a trowel to make a hole and set the plants at the same level as they were growing in the trays.

4. In milder regions, plant the cloves in well-prepared soil, use as much organic matter as possible to assist with drainage. Simply push the cloves into the soil so that the tip of each one is just below the surface. Space each clove about 10cm (4in) apart. If planting in rows, space each row 45cm (18in) apart.

5. Roots will emerge from the base of the clove and green shoots from the tip. The shoots may die back over the winter if they are exposed to super cold weather, but don't fret. They will re-grow in the spring.

6. It is a good idea to mulch the ground after planting to keep down weeds.

7. Grow your garlic in full sun - garlic needs to grow quickly in order to produce good sized bulbs. Pick a site that is not prone to water-logging, this will ensure the bulbs do not rot over winter.

8. Dig in some sand (from your garden centre) at this stage to improve the drainage even further.

9. If the soil has been prepared as described above, just sit back and watch the plants grow - they are almost completely free of disease, and their only requirement is watering if the conditions become very dry.

10. Apart from this, their only other requirement is to be kept free of weeds and watered in very dry conditions. They will produce green foliage starting around April time. If it's dry for long periods, the cloves will not swell and the resulting crop will have a short storage life.

11. It is a good idea to plant garlic in a raised bed – easier to weed and manage, which is where I grow mine.

Garlic Harvesting Tips

1. The key to harvesting garlic is knowing when it is ripe. Harvest too early and the bulbs will be small, harvest too late and the bulb will have split making harvest difficult and the cloves of low quality (they will have commenced their growing cycle for next year).

2. Garlic is ready for harvesting when most of the foliage has turned a yellowy-brown color - this will be around mid-August time.

3. Problems may occur in wet summers - the leaves may only have started to turn yellow but if the garlic is left in wet ground at this stage, the bulbs will very quickly become diseased.

4. For this reason a second method is used to determine what stage they have reached. If the weather is wet in early August, pull up one bulb and see how many sheaths (very thin papery layers around the bulb) you can peel off the bulb.

5. If there are only three, harvest the bulbs, if there are four or more, wait another two weeks or until most of the leaves have turned brown.

6. When harvesting garlic bulbs, gently ease them out of the ground with the assistance of a trowel to loosen the surrounding soil - be careful not to bruise them with the trowel because they will then not keep for long.

7. Kept in an open container in a cool, dry place, dried, unbroken garlic bulbs will last for up to a month or more. Separated cloves will keep for up to 10 days.

.. and finally (garlic)

As mentioned above, garlic is absurdly easy to plant and care for, and it takes up so little ground that even those with very small gardens can raise enough to be self-sufficient in garlic for a good part of the year.

All you have to do is choose the right varieties; plant at the right time, in the right soil and then enjoy a fruitful harvest.

Be careful with wild garlic, as it may try to take over your garden or raised bed if you don't control it – not a bad problem to have really!

Garlic is easy and fun to grow, even if you're not a very experienced gardener. You also get the reward of eating your home-grown garlic crop.

Now for more tasty recipes..

My Top 10 Recipes with Garlic

When garlic cloves are cooked or baked whole, the flavor mellows into a sweet, almost nutty flavor that hardly resembles any form of pungency. This nutty flavor makes a surprisingly nice addition to desserts, such as brownies or even ice cream, but this is an acquired taste!

One raw garlic clove, finely minced or pressed releases more flavor than a dozen cooked whole cloves.

Regarding the flavor of garlic - the smaller you cut it, the stronger the flavor. Chopping finely or pressing a clove exposes more surfaces to the air, causing a chemical reaction to produce that strong aroma and potent flavor.

Use roast whole bulbs or individual cloves to serve with roast meat; fry (slowly, for just a couple of minutes) to use as the base for sauces, casseroles, soups.

21.   <u>Roast Garlic and Lemon Soup</u>

This soup is full of flavor, combining two of my favorite ingredients: garlic and lemon. Although it takes a bit of time to make, it's well worth the effort!

Preparation	Cooking	Serving
30 mins	90 mins	120 mins

INGREDIENTS

1 large fresh garlic

2 tsp olive oil

2 cups chopped yellow onion

1 tbsp finely chopped fresh flat-leaf parsley

1/2 tbsp finely chopped fresh thyme

12-15 peeled garlic cloves

4 cups of vegetable stock

2 tbsp fresh lemon juice

1/2 cup of your preferred fresh milk

A handful of fresh parsley sprigs and lemon zest, for garnish

PREPARATION

Preheat the oven to 175°C/350°F.

Drizzle the garlic head with olive oil, wrap with foil and place in oven for 1 hour, or until lightly golden and very soft and fragrant. Let garlic cool until it can be handled.

Using your fingers, gently squeeze the cloves to release them from their skins into a bowl, and set aside. Discard the skins.

In a heavy-bottom pot or saucepan, heat the olive oil over medium high heat.

Add onions, parsley and thyme, cook until onions are just softened (3 mins).

Add the fresh and roasted garlic, and cook, stirring often, until the onions are translucent, about 3-4 minutes more.

Add vegetable stock and lemon juice, turn down heat and simmer, covered, for 35 mins, until garlic is very tender.

Working 1-2 cups at a time, process the soup in a blender, transferring the soup to another bowl or saucepan. (nb - never fill a blender with hot liquid more than half-way full and make sure the lid is on securely before processing.)

Transfer the puréed soup to the saucepan, add the milk and salt, and return the mixture to a low simmer.

SERVING

Garnish with fresh parsley and lemon zest and serve.

22.   Roast Lamb with Rosemary and Garlic

If you have time, stud the lamb a day in advance to allow the flavors to really permeate the meat (this is so good I might include in my Rosemary book too).

Preparation	Cooking	Serving
15 mins	105 mins	120 mins

INGREDIENTS

1 leg of lamb weighing 2.5kg/5lb 8oz

1 garlic bulb

1 bunch fresh rosemary

1 tbsp vegetable oil

2 carrots, cut into large chunks

1 onion, cut into quarters

1 glass red wine (about 150ml)

1.2L beef or lamb stock

PREPARATION

Stud the lamb with the garlic and rosemary - use a sharp pointed knife, make 30 small incisions all over the meat.

Peel 4 garlic cloves, thinly slice them and prod a slice into each incision.

Pull off small sprigs of rosemary and push into the incisions too. If done in advance, cover the lamb well and refrigerate. Remove from the fridge 1 hr before roasting.

Heat a large frying pan, add a little oil and brown the lamb all over. Scatter the carrot, onion, remaining garlic and rosemary in a large roasting tin, pour in wine and stock, then place the browned lamb in the tin.

Roast in preheated oven at 190°C/370° for 100 mins. Turn the lamb halfway through so by the time it is cooked, each side has been in the stock.

When cooked, remove the lamb and allow to rest in a warm place covered in foil for about 30 mins.

Prepare gravy. Pour stock through a sieve into a saucepan to remove all the vegetables and herbs. The stock should be rich, slightly thick and have a great lamb flavor.

Reduce it a little on the hob if you want to concentrate the flavor, skimming off any fat that comes to the surface.

SERVING

Serve lamb with the gravy, potatoes, leeks and butternut squash.

23.   <u>Roast Parsnips with Garlic</u>

This easy recipe will make you think about roast parsnips in a whole new way.

Preparation	Cooking	Serving
10 mins	50 mins	60 mins

INGREDIENTS

1kg small parsnips, each 100-125g

200ml sunflower oil

6 garlic cloves, unpeeled

15g butter

2 long fresh rosemary sprigs, halved

PREPARATION

Cut each parsnip in half lengthways.

Drop into a pan of boiling slightly salted water and cook for about 5 mins.

Drain the parsnips well in a colander, wait for the steam to die down.

Meanwhile, pour the sunflower oil into a roasting tin and heat in the oven at 190°C/375°F /gas 5 for 5 minutes, or until the oil is really hot.

Slightly crush (or chop) the garlic cloves under the flat side of a large knife.

Add the parsnips to the tin, toss well in the hot oil then pour away the excess oil – this ensures the parsnips are dry and crisp, not greasy.

Dot the parsnips with the butter and scatter over the rosemary and garlic.

Roast for 30 minutes.

Increase the oven temperature to 200°C/fan180°C/gas 6.

Turn the parsnips and roast for a further 20 minutes or until golden and crispy.

SERVING

Serve with any meat dish, or with a cold meat platter.

24.   <u>Garlic Chicken Breast with Cheese</u>

Grated cheese is sprinkled on top of the chicken breast the last 5 minutes of cooking (optional).

Preparation	Cooking	Serving
20 mins	40 mins	60 mins

INGREDIENTS

4 boneless skinless chicken breasts

1/3 cup butter, melted

2 tbsp minced garlic (approx)

2 cloves fresh garlic, 1/2 tsp seasoning salt

3/4 cup seasoned dry bread crumb (seasoned or plain)

1/2 cup finely grated cheddar cheese

1/4 cup freshly grated parmesan cheese

Shredded cheddar or mozzarella cheese

1/2 cup beef broth, 1/2 cup frozen peas

PREPARATION

Preheat oven to 175°C/350°F.

Butter an 11 x 7-inch pan (if using more than 4 breasts use a larger pan).

In a bowl, combine melted butter with 1 tsp minced garlic, and chopped or pressed garlic.

In another bowl, combine the dry breadcrumbs with 1/2 cup finely grated cheddar cheese, Parmesan cheese 1 tsp garlic powder and coarse ground black pepper.

Dip chicken in butter mixture, then in crumb mixture.

Place in prepared pan and bake uncovered for 35-45 minutes or until cooked through, larger breasts may take more time (placing the chicken on a rack in a pan will produce an extra crispy crust).

Top with shredded cheddar or mozzarella the last 5 minutes of cooking (this is only optional.

SERVING

Serve with roast, fried or mashed potatoes and steamed vegetables.

Salt and pepper to taste.

25.   Garlic Roasted Pork

Fatty cuts of pork with the skin on are crisp and savory, but lean cuts like pork loin can be just as tasty with the intense garlic rub in this recipe.

Preparation	Cooking	Serving
15 mins	70 mins	85 mins

INGREDIENTS

6 cloves garlic, peeled and crushed or chopped finely

2 tbsp extra-virgin olive oil

1 tbsp dried oregano

1 tsp paprika

1/2 tsp freshly ground pepper

2 pound boneless pork loin, trimmed

1 tsp salt

PREPARATION

Combine garlic, oil, oregano, paprika, salt and pepper in a food processor or blender and purée.

Rub the pork all over with seasoning mix, and wrap tightly with plastic wrap or place in a large sealable plastic bag.

Marinate in the refrigerator for at least 20 minutes or ideally 1 day.

Preheat oven to 350°F/175°C.

Remove the pork from the plastic and place in a shallow roasting pan.

Roast, uncovered for 50 minutes to 1 hour.

SERVING

Allow to rest for 10 minutes.

Slice and serve with rice and salad, or potatoes and steamed vegetables.

26.   <u>Garlic Chicken</u>

Simple to make, just dip and bake - garlic goodness in a breaded chicken dish.

Preparation	Cooking	Serving
20 mins	35 mins	55 mins

INGREDIENTS

4 skinless, boneless chicken breast halves

2 tsp crushed or chopped garlic

1/4 cup olive oil

1/4 cup dry bread crumbs

1 tbsp mixed herbs

1/4 cup grated Parmesan cheese

PREPARATION

Preheat oven to 425°F (220°C).

Warm the garlic and olive oil in a small dish to blend the flavors.

In a separate dish, combine the bread crumbs, herbs and Parmesan cheese.

Dip the chicken breasts in the olive oil and garlic mixture, then into the bread crumb mixture.

Place in a shallow baking dish.

Bake in the preheated oven for 30 to 35 mins, until no longer pink and juices run clear.

SERVING

Serve with choice of rice or fries or mashed potatoes and vegetables or salad.

27.   Peppery Garlic Prawns

This really packs a punch with all of the black pepper - cut back on the pepper to tone it down a bit if you wish.

Preparation	Cooking	Serving
10 mins	60 mins	75 mins

INGREDIENTS

4 cloves garlic, crushed

1/2 tsp salt

1 tsp crushed black peppercorns

1 tsp fresh lemon juice

2 tbsp brandy*

1 lb. raw medium-sized shrimp, shelled, de-veined and split (tails on or off)**

1-2 tbsp olive oil

2 tbsp fresh chopped fresh parsley

PREPARATION

Mix together the crushed garlic, salt, crushed peppercorns, lemon juice and brandy.

Add the shrimp and marinate for at least an hour (or better overnight in the fridge).

Heat a heavy skillet over medium high heat and add olive oil.

Add shrimp and garlic mixture and cook quickly, tossing shrimp.

(The longer the shrimp has been marinating, the less time it takes to cook).

Cook until the shrimp has turned transparent (only 2-3 mins).

SERVING

Garnish with chopped parsley. Season with salt and pepper.

CW Tips:

The recipe also calls for a tablespoon of *brandy. I think this is an essential ingredient for the recipe. But if you simply cannot cook with alcohol, add a dab of butter to the olive oil. It will change the flavor of the finished dish, but it should still taste great.

28.   <u>Spinach with Sesame and Garlic</u>

A Korean take on spinach, with the spinach wilted in sesame oil with garlic, and sprinkled with toasted sesame seeds.

Preparation	Cooking	Serving
15 mins	25 mins	40 mins

INGREDIENTS

3 tbsp dark sesame oil

1 tbsp minced garlic

1 lb fresh spinach, washed and drained, excess water squeezed out, large stems removed and discarded, leaves roughly chopped

1 tbsp sugar

1 tbsp soy sauce (use gluten-free soy sauce for gluten-free version)

1 tbsp toasted sesame seeds

PREPARATION

Toast the sesame seeds. Heat a stick-free skillet on medium high.

Add raw seeds and use a wooden spoon to stir. The seeds may make a popping noise and jump up. Stir constantly until they begin to brown and smell like they are toasted. Remove into a separate bowl as soon as they are done.

Heat 2 tbsp of sesame oil in large skillet over medium heat.

Once the oil is hot, add the garlic.

As soon as the garlic begins to sizzle, add the spinach and cook, stirring occasionally, until the spinach is completely wilted.

Turn the heat to low.

Stir in the sugar and soy sauce.

Now remove from the heat. Add salt to taste.

SERVING

Serve hot or cold, drizzled with the remaining sesame oil and sprinkled with more sesame seeds.

CW Tips:

If you are using bagged baby spinach, the presoaking is not necessary, as that spinach is pretty clean. The spinach you get in bunches from the farmers market can have a lot of dirt at the root ball that needs to be washed out before you use it.

29.   Chicken Kiev

Chicken Kiev is one of those old favourites that everyone loves, especially the kids.

Preparation	Cooking	Serving
15 mins	15 mins	30 mins

INGREDIENTS

2 x 75g boneless, skinless chicken breasts

40g unsalted butter, at room temperature

4 tbsp chopped parsley

2 cloves garlic, crushed

5 tbsp fresh breadcrumbs

1 tbsp parmesan, freshly grated

1 tbsp plain flour, seasoned with salt and pepper

1 egg, beaten.   1-2 tbsp vegetable oil

PREPARATION

Using a small knife, horizontally cut a pocket into each chicken breast.

Mix together the butter, parsley, garlic with salt and pepper to taste.

Spoon the mixture into the pocket of each chicken breast.

Stir together the breadcrumbs and Parmesan.

Dust the chicken breasts in the seasoned flour then the beaten egg and finally, roll in the breadcrumb mixture.

Heat the vegetable oil in a large frying pan

Cook the chicken for 5-6 minutes on each side until golden brown and cooked through.

SERVING

Serve with lemon potato wedges and a crisp green salad.

30.   Caesar Salad

Probably the most popular restaurant salad in the US, with plenty of variations around the theme of romaine lettuce, garlic, Parmesan, and croutons.

Preparation	Cooking	Serving
30 mins	0 mins	35 mins

INGREDIENTS

1/2 cup extra virgin olive oil

4 cloves fresh garlic, peeled, smashed, then minced

1 baguette, preferably a day old, sliced thin

1/4 cup freshly juiced lemon juice (plus more to taste)

4 oz Parmesan cheese, grated

1 tsp anchovy paste, or 1-2 anchovies, smashed and minced

2 eggs

4-6 small heads of romaine lettuce, wilted leaves discarded

PREPARATION

In large bowl, whisk together the olive oil and garlic.

Let sit for half an hour. While the oil is sitting, make the croutons.

Spread the baguette slices out over a baking sheet (may need to do in batches), lined with parchment paper.

Brush or spray with olive oil (or melted butter).

Broil for a couple of mins until the tops are lightly browned.

Remove and let cool.

The steps up until this point can be made in advance.

Add anchovies and eggs to the oil garlic mixture and whisk until creamy.

Add sea salt and black pepper to taste, and 1/4 cup of lemon juice.

Whisk in half of the Parmesan cheese.

Taste, add more lemon juice to taste. The lemon should give an edge to the dressing, but not overwhelm it.

Tear off chunks of lettuce (do not use a knife to cut). Add to the oil mixture and toss until coated.

Add the rest of the Parmesan cheese

Coarsely chop the toasted bread and add (with crumbs from chopping) to the salad. Toss.

SERVING

Dish out and serve immediately.

CW Tips:

If you have a concern about the raw eggs called for in this recipe, you can use pasteurized eggs, or you can coddle the eggs first by immersing them in boiling water for 1 minute, before cracking them open.

4 - Colin's Handy Conversion Table

Oz	Grams	Fl. Oz.	ml	Cup	tbsp.	tsp.
1/2	14	1/2	15	1/16	1	3
1	28	1	30	1/8	2	6
1 1/2	43	1 1/2	44	3/16	3	9
2	57	2	59	1/4	4	12
2 1/2	71	2 1/2	74	5/16	5	15
3	85	3	89	3/8	6	18
3 1/2	99	3 1/2	104	7/16	7	21
4	113	4	118	1/2	8	24
4 1/2	128	4 1/2	133	9/16	9	27
5	142	5	148	5/8	10	30
5 1/2	156	5 1/2	163	11/16	11	33
6	170	6	177	6/8	12	36
6 1/2	184	6 1/2	192	13/16	13	39
7	199	7	207	7/8	14	42
7 1/2	213	7 1/2	222	15/16	15	45
8	227	8	237	1	16	48

To be exact - 1 oz = 28.35 grams = 1 fl. oz = 29.57 ml = 1/8 cup = 2 tbsp. = 6 tsp.

Using a fan oven you need to reduce the oven temperature in a recipe by 20 degrees.

References

I compiled this book from the first three books in my series all about herbs and spices, which evolved from my experience growing and cooking with ginger, chives, and garlic – with a few favorite recipes.

Look out for new books in the series, and special deals for my regular readers. Visit my website –

www.howtogrowherbgarden.com, or email me with any questions on herbs or gardening.

Thanks and Happy Herbing –

colin@howtogrowherbgarden.com

www.altmedicine.about.com

www.eatingwell.com

A final quote from Colin:

"Make the effort and start growing your own fresh herbs and spices – easier than you think, very rewarding and enjoy the

Printed in Great Britain
by Amazon.co.uk, Ltd.,
Marston Gate.